LOVE IS...

A Collection of
Poetry, Spoken Word,
and Short Stories

Valerie L. McDowell

Editor

LOVE IS...

A COLLECTION OF POETRY, SPOKEN WORD, AND SHORT STORIES

VALERIE L. MCDOWELL, EDITOR

Publisher: Power2Excel Agency, LLC

Unless otherwise noted, Scripture taken from THE MESSAGE Copyright ©1993, 1994, 1995, 1996, 2000, 2001, 2002. Used by permission of NavPress Publishing Group.

Each poem is the individual work and intellectual property of each author.

ISBN: 979-8-9860191-2-3(Paperback Edition)

www.bookcoachexcel-erator.com

Printed in the United States of America

ACKNOWLEDGMENTS

I want to honor the amazing humans who create from their soul, their lives, their disappointments, and their dreams. This Collection is a sweet Thank You! for sharing time and space with me on planet Earth. And whether this is you first publication or one of many; and just in case you never publish another thing, I celebrate the contribution you made to this project and call out your name here:

Gerri Aldridge

Betty Badgett

Rocio L. Baker

Jermain Barnes

Lynn Brown

Cheryl Crockett

Cari Davis

Darlene Gibson

Debrina Hall James

Valrie Yee Logan

Valerie L. McDowell

Chatone Morrison

Linda Peterson

Ozetta V. Posey

Martita Robbins

Marsha Reeves Jews

Octavia Smith

Arnita Sydnor

Sandra Thomas

Annie Veyakhone

Linda Jones Vickers

Elouise D. Woodard

LOVE IS...

A COLLECTION OF POETRY, SPOKEN WORD, AND SHORT STORIES
VALERIE L. MCDOWELL, EDITOR

TABLE OF CONTENTS

Poetry

CLOSE UP & PERSONAL - A LOVE POEM DURING COVID

by Chatone Morrison

What I really want to do is sit and eat ice cream and drink lukewarm
coffee and stand outside of a store window and watch television.
The way my parents did when they were young and technology was
new when you had to walk on the street or visit someone just to get it.
And I want to touch someone's face, their lips, their cheeks
and see them laugh.
Close up and personal and be myself and scream while reciting
poetry.
Walking in the park, doing a live stream and not worry about this
spit that slips from my unmasked mouth.
I want to see your eyes the way your lashes flutter without the
presence of tear drops.
I want to smell your teeth and see the gray hair tucked behind your
ears.
Close up and personal.
I want to walk in your shoes and feel your arm on the pillow and
touch the paper after you read it in the morning
And I want morning to be just morning without news and numbers
and flattening the curves and mourning.
What I really want to do is everything and nothing much and see the
present as a gift.
It really is.
And smile at every stranger I meet and walk down on the street
running my hands across every fence to finally sit in our favorite
park, on our favorite bench beneath our favorite pink and white tree.
What I really want to do is just silently stare at you while you
silently stare at me.

THE BEST PART
by Martita Robbins

The best part of my day is the end
The beating within your chest is a soundtrack flowing
through my ears
A lullaby that seduces me to sleep

The warmth and weight of your hands holding me like a
security blanket
I am comfortable in your space
I want to cherish each moment

My biggest fear is that there's the possibility that each
time is the last time
So I make you my favorite habit
My favorite pastime

MOTHER'S NATURE
by Jermain Barnes

A storm comes, chaos pursue
The rain comes and all is blue
The fire comes near, destruction is clear
The flood comes to put all in fear
Mother nature might be severe
My mother's nature is all sincere
With storm comes peace
With rain new beginning
With fire new horizon
With flood fresh landscape
Mother nature might cause concern
It's from my mother's nature we can all learn

LOVE IS..
by Darlene Gibson

Love is a beautiful connection shared between married couples,
sharing joy and pain with one another.
Love is also a great experience found in the relationships of
friends, family members,
And in a sister, father, brother, or mother.

When you love someone, there is no limit to the battles you will
fight and endure,
As long as the connections, relationships, and sincerities are secure.

It takes patience, commitment, and reciprocity to grow.
Change and forgiveness are sure signs you know.

The best part of love happens when you take the time to
learn and explore,
Being intentional, exceptional, and making time for sure.

Knowing and loving, God's love is the key to learning to love
properly.
God's love empowers us and guides us to express such a
commitment.
And once we develop a relationship and become engrafted to our
Heavenly Father,
He can help us give all our feelings and passions to His will to gain
Holy Ghost power.

A BLANKET OF LOVE
by Sandra Thomas

The sunrays fall upon her frail withered body,
as she lies in the desert of loneliness.
Her parched dry lips taste the saltiness of her blood,
when she breaks into a sweat that floods her chest.

Would there be any relief for her?
Can she feel the warmth of his love once again?
The summer heat has darkened her face and a veil her eyes
She sees a reflection of his picture, from a-far, shining brighter
His countenance is radiant.

Suddenly! Appearing full clarity, she can taste and see his
goodness,
Covered by his ravishing love, a ravenous coolness poured-over
body.
A blanket, a blanket of love covering her from the sun,
She laid on her back, afraid to move.
Awaken! Awaken! Oh, my darling from your place of slumber,
he whispers words of love.

Approaching, he picks her up and promises never to withdraw his
voice from her-
should she remember, and desire his warm soothing strokes.
Strokes, of mercy, strokes of love.
She is covered by his blanket of love.

LOVE IS
by Linda Peterson

Love is caring.

Love is sharing the good times and the bad,

A look, a touch, a wink, a sigh,

Love is a hand to hold,

Love is hanging on when the going gets rough,

Love is sometimes defying the odds.

Love is building a life together.

Love is being there for each other, no matter what.

LOVE IS
by Gerri Aldridge

Love is when you write a special note to your mom after she has transitioned.
Today Mom all eyes are on "you"!
Why? Because you always left a favorable
impression on anyone who graced your presence.
Your kind words and deeds at
Mount Carmel Baptist Church and
throughout your community are too numerous to mention.
However, I am sure the people who have
benefited from your unselfish acts know who they are.
I want you to know that I will use your
fine attributes as a guide in my life,
such as volunteering my time, using my special gifts and talent
to help others, but today, all eyes are on "you"'
Harriet Tubman, Zora Neale Hurston, and
Coretta Scott King were great women in Black History
but today, all eyes are on "you".
I am especially grateful to you for all the joy and wisdom you
brought to our family.
I will never forget all the many places we traveled both in the
U.S., the Caribbean, and
Throughout the United States.
But today, all eyes are on "you".

Rest in Heaven!
Your daughter, Gerri

IT WAS ALWAYS ABOUT YOU
by Cari Davis

It was always about you.
Each time I dressed up "like" in "love's" clothes and made
myself believe "like" was all I deserved.
It was always about you.
Every time I experienced pain and sadness it was so I would
be able to recognize your love when it came.
It was always about you.
Time spent surrendering all of me to God to make room for
the love you would bring.
It was always about you.
The one I didn't know I needed.
God not only prepared you for me now. He's preparing you to
be who I will need.
It is with a grateful, awakened, and anointed
heart that I say Lord thank you for blessing me with you!
Because, it was always about you!

Corinthians 13:3 -13 - That's Love!

...No matter what I say, what I believe, and what I do, I'm
bankrupt without love.

Love never gives up.
Love cares more for others than for self.
Love doesn't want what it doesn't have.
Love doesn't strut,
Doesn't have a swelled head,
Doesn't force itself on others,
Isn't always "me first,"
Doesn't fly off the handle,
Doesn't keep score of the sins of others,
Doesn't revel when others grovel,
Takes pleasure in the flowering of truth,
Puts up with anything,
Trusts God always,
Always looks for the best,
Never looks back,
But keeps going to the end.
(The Message Bible)

LOVE IS A CHOICE
by Debrina Hall James

Love is a choice they say
Can that be really true?
For many believe it's just a feeling you have
When you care enough to give all of you.

Love is a choice they say
Not solely based on feelings at all
For feelings will often come and go
Love is in for the long haul.

Love is a choice they say
That goes beyond feelings that may arise
Feelings of pleasure, giddiness, and joy
Nervous excitement and butterflies.

Love is a choice they say
That will endure the test of time
Whereas feelings will often fluctuate
And change at the drop of a dime.

Love is a choice they say
It's not based on what others do
Love is a choice to continue to love
Regardless of what others may do to you.

17

YOUR PRESENCE

by Cari Davis

Your presence in my life is an answered prayer.

Your presence in my life touches me in ways
That cause me to want to be a better version of myself.

Your presence in my life reminds me often by what
you do and say, that I am loved.

Your presence in my life allows God's guidance
And direction be known when we gather together.

Your presence in my life has blessed me
With a sister and friend.

Thank you for the encouragement, assignments,
And your unconditional, authentic love.

Your presence in my life continues
To bless me.

And this I pray:
That your love may abound yet more and more.
Philippians 1:9 (The Message)

LOVE IS
by Ozetta V. Posey

Love is dark
Love takes you to the park
Love is cold
Love makes you feel bold
Love leaves you weak
Love makes you peak

Love is a mix of emotions
Love is like a potion
Which can leave you sitting in the ocean
Love is.

LOVE IS
by Octavia Smith

Love is blind
Some people talk about it
Some people cry about it
Some people break things over it
They even wrote a song about it,
but they say Love is blind.
Some people kill for it
Some even went to jail because of it
Still they say love is blind.

Truly the light is sweet, and a pleasant thing it is for
the eyes to behold the sun.
Ecclesiastes 4:7 (The Message)

SUMMER LOVE, 2009
By Lynn Brown

My heart is anxious
Summer Love, where you hidin?
Sing me a love song!

I like my lips to know
They're not being Jived
So kiss me a rainbow!

HURRY
by Lynn Brown
I keep yearning for you
to be inside my arms
Hurry up and come inside.

CHERYL CROCKETT HAIKU

Cheryl's Everyday Haiku ~ (Feb. 13, 2013)

HAIKU #45

Cupid plans his flight
Hopefuls get bulls-eye tattoos
And stand very still.

Cheryl's Everyday #Haiku * Day 04

Haiku Poem

His kiss was sincere
It moved me so deeply
I woke up from my dream.

Cheryl's Everyday #Haiku * Day 29

Haiku Poem

one broken heart
two end a relationship
hidden third party

Haiku

he wants to kiss me
don't let this moment end
my Uber arrives

© 2018 Cheryl L. Crockett

Haiku

February woes
Some want their own Valentine
Others a groundhog

© 2022 Cheryl L. Crockett

SPOKEN
Word

A LOVE SUPREME
by Valerie L. McDowell

Out of this world.

That's what it felt like. The first time I experienced true love.
I had been seeking Him. Wanting Him to invade my place of
being. To overwhelm my existence. To fill every empty void,
every empty place that I had struggled to fill for so long. I had
tried it all. Knew that I had all the answers. But all of it - the
drugs, the sex, the money, fame, knowledge, influence - it all left
me the same. But I kept seeking and buying and still was never
satisfied. I had the money and the toys. Had traveled all around
the world. But they all left this hole that only One could fill.
But I could not let it go. There was more to this than what I had.
So I kept at it. Seeking. Desiring his presence. Longing for the
love that would last a lifetime.

When Suddenly He showed up.

And I WAS NOT READY FOR IT. I mean, who can be?

Nothing on earth can prepare you for a love that ... that
encompasses all.

That surpasses all understanding. A love for which there are
not enough words to convey. A love that is beyond experiences,
beyond memories, beyond heartaches and pain. Beyond joys and
triumphs. A love that transcends time and space.

That propels itself through 42 generations to come rescue me.
To show me the way. A love that steps inside the confinement
of flesh. A love that lays down its life for me. A love that rises
above every obstacle just for me.

A Love Supreme.

LOVE JUST IS ...
by Marsha Reeves-Jews

"Love is Patient, Love is Kind. It's not Jealous, Pompous, Inflated.
It's not Rude, does not seek Its Own Interests, not Quick-
Tempered, doesn't Brood over Injury or Rejoice Over Wrongdoing
but Rejoices with the Truth. It Bears ALL things, Believes ALL
things, Hopes ALL things, Endures ALL things. Love Never Fails!"
(1 Corinthians 13:6-8)

Love comes in so many forms.
Love involves all levels of our being,
yet it is very difficult to suffer through during difficult times.
Love allows you to be available when needed, creates an environment
to put our feelings last, and causes our egos to decrease.
Love encompasses our entire spirit, our very being.
Love is all consuming and has the ability to cause immeasurable pain
that cuts to the depth of our very being and eats away at our very core;
while simultaneously creating a euphoria unlike anything our hearts,
minds, body, and spirit can explain or express.
Once ignited Love is all inclusive, it cannot be contained or controlled.

YOU ARE
by Valerie L. McDowell

You are a perfect conduit of the Father's love, flowing effortlessly through time and space. Your love for me envelops my very soul, halting my thoughts, and capturing my wildest imagination. I celebrate the song your heart sings when you are in my presence and the joy that overwhelms me when I see your smile. Oh! I am the most blessed of God's creation where his perfect love abounds, circumventing the channels of logic and reason and grasping the light of eternal peace, miraculously lifting every burden, every circumstance, every yoke. To be loved by you is a most wondrous, exhilarating, unimaginable testament to the greatest love affair of them all.

BROKEN
By Arnita Sydnor

Look into my eyes; can you see the broken pieces?
Torn, twisted, confused, darkness, anger, and unknown faces,
Tell me what you see.

My hair is thinning, skin falling off my bones
the blood running; slowly through my veins, heart full of holes,
I reach out my hand, trying to grasp a grip, extension
growing and growing, the rubber band, a never-ending stretch
Finally grab a hold, I've captured a soul, only to find that it's been
broken.

I've searched so long to find parts of me, broken,
Tell me, can you see what i see, a reflection, a mere existence
of what I'd like to be, dreams, desires, if only in my reach
help me find the broken pieces - Broken.
This pain is deep; I'm trying to tell you that it's me fighting me

TO MY FOREVER VALENTINE!!

by Betty Badgett

LOVE IS SITTING ACROSS THE DINING ROOM TABLE,
OUR EYES LOCKED ON EACH OTHER
AS WE ENJOY OUR MORNING CUP OF COFFEE.

LOVE IS HELPING YOU SLIP ON YOUR
PANTS, ONE LEG AT A TIME,
AS YOU HOLD ON TO ME.
I HELP YOU TO THE CAR,
AND OFF WE GO AGAIN
AS WE DO EVERY WEEK,
TO GET YOUR CHEMO TREATMENT.

LOVE IS BEING TOGETHER FORTY-FOUR YEARS,
RAISING OUR SON AND DAUGHTER, TOGETHER.

THIS FIGHT WE'RE IN RIGHT NOW
IS A TEST OF SAID LOVE.
I'M PROUD TO SAY,
THAT EVEN IN THE MIDST
OF THIS PAINFUL SITTUATION,
LOVE IS WINING.
MY LOVE FOR YOU AND
MY EMPATHY FOR WHAT IS HAPPENING TO YOU
IS STRONGER THAN EVER,
AND SO IS MY LOVE.

LOVE IS LYING ON A HARD RECLINER CHAIR NEXT
TO YOUR BEDSIDE IN THE HOSPITAL.

HOLDING YOUR HAND WHEN I SENSE YOU'RE SCARED.

LOVE WAS WHISPERING GOODBYE
IN YOUR EAR, THANKING YOU FOR
ALL THE JOY YOU BROUGHT INTO
MY LIFE OVER THE YEARS.

LOVE WAS RELEASING YOU BACK TO THE
GOD THAT CREATED YOU AND LOVED YOU.

LOVE WAS BEING WITH YOU
AND HAVING YOUR BACK,
FROM THE DIAGNOSIS
TO THE MOMENT YOU TOOK YOUR LAST BREATH.

LOVE IS NAVIGATING MY WAY
THROUGH THIS LIFE
WITHOUT YOUR EARTHLY PRESENCE.
FINDING PLACES WHERE I FIT IN.
STARTING OVER IN A NEW STATE,
MAKING NEW FRIENDS
AND GETTING UP OUT OF BED
EVERY MORNING,
REMEMBERING YOU
AND STILL LOVING YOU.

TRUE LOVE NEVER DIE'S, IT JUST
LIVES ON AND TAKES UP A SPECIAL
PLACE IN YOUR HEART
AND BECOMES PRECIOUS MEMORIES
STORED FOR ETERNITY IN YOUR MIND.

SILENT MOTHERLY LOVE
By Rocio L. Baker

What is "Love"? Oh my!
I asked myself last night,
While sitting on my white rocking chair.
Clear sky and pleasant view,
Surrounded by a crepuscular light.
Colored flowers listening,
Remaining silent from start to finish.
Silence inspired my words,
This calm crowd reminded me of my Mother,
Whose love was silent but mighty.

As time went by, I thought about "Love,"
Love in the world, love in the community,
Love as a couple, love in all its forms.
Out of the blue, oh my! I felt motionless.
A narcissistic spirit enslaved my thoughts,
And did not allow me to escape.
I surrendered and followed,
Hypnotized by his might.

I am not vain, not at all! My friends,
But this time, only this time,
I wanted to concentrate on my life.
I surrounded my thinking in one person,
One unique and special person.
I allowed myself to cry out loud,

31

And self-center one hundred ten percent of the Time
On my "Silent Motherly Love."

The love for my mother is so great. Oh my!
Raising five children on her own,
Without ever complaining,
Without ever crying. Can you do that?
She took good care of us, you know,
every day, every night, every second,
And every minute of her life.
Without stopping, she allowed us to grow tall.
From seed to tree, she was there,
Every step of the way and beyond....
Caring from dusk to dawn,
Without breaking in half.
How did she do that?
You would ask....
Well, I think I know!
It was the power of her
Immense "Silent Motherly Love."

My heart thanks her for her sacrifice.
With her soft voice, step by step,
She built a beloved place.
A site with mud bricks and corrugated iron,
So nobody could breeze in and destroy it.
It protected us every day from the dangers
Of the mysterious, colorful jungle.

She, my Mother, the queen of the castle,
Deserves not one, not two, not three,
But a hundred golden crowns.
She differs from the rest, you know...
Do you want to know why?
It is because she owns this special "Silent Motherly Love."

She did not have a college degree,
But she was without a question
The wisest woman there was.
She sent me to school,
Along with my sisters,
And my brother as well.
They finished high school,
but I can proudly say,
"I am the first in my family
With the highest degree there is."
Thanks to her expectations.
How about her expectations?
Let me just tell you this.
Her expectations, oh my!
Were the highest in the hood.
Because of her invisible intelligence,
She is my "Silent Motherly Love."

My Mother's love was wordless.
It is not because she didn't talk,
Not at all, my friends.

She expressed herself well, I'll say.
It was because expressing her feelings
Didn't come easy for her.

Besides, her active daily routine did not have
a beginning, nor a middle, or an end.
With her continuous actions, which occurred daily,
Weekly, monthly, and yearly.
She showed her love for us.
As a child, I didn't fully understand
Some of her actions,
But as I grew older, I comprehended
That she had to make hard decisions,
Because she wanted the best for all of us.
For this and other reasons,
She is my "Silent Motherly Love."

She was resilient then,
And she is resilient now.
She suffered, I know,
But her heart showed compassion.
Oh, my! And still does nowadays.
Oh! Dear mother, mother, mother,
I can see your power radiating all over.
Your inner soul is gold, precious, precious gold.
You drew strength where you did not have.
No matter how hard the storm you faced,
You kept going and going.

You controlled the steering wheel,
Without knowing how,
And crashed many times, I know.
But one thing is for sure,
You always emerged stronger.
Oh querida! "Silent Motherly Love."

It is 2:00 am now.
I am still awake.
Day dawn will arrive soon,
to touch my face with a flare of cool air.
I might take a quick nap,
but my agenda has no beginning nor an end.
What is love? I asked my audience again.
Since they didn't respond,
All I could say as I fell fast asleep was,
"Love is Silent, Motherly Love."

MY LOVE AFFAIR WITH WORDS
By Valerie L. McDowell

You see I have this love affair with words,

There's just something about the way you say them or use them or don't.

I remember when I was a child; how I used to just sit and read the dictionary, looking for words I didn't know. How I would practice them, rehearsing them over and over and over again, enunciating each syllable, loving how easily they would slip and slide and sometimes jam off my tongue.

With words like omniligent or superfluous, vacuous or soliloquy, jejune or loquacious, feckless or facetious, epiphany or evanescent, diffident or deciduous –

Can't you just hear it?

And not just the ones that seemed difficult words, but the easy ones too, or so I thought, like love and hate, mine and yours, his and hers, why and why not, when and how long –

You know those words

And then there are those words from long ago that just make me want to stand up and shout

Words like straightway and lo, verily, behold and surely, nevertheless and forever,

Yes – how I love them

And it started quite a while ago,

So long ago in fact that you really have to start at the beginning for

In the beginning was the Word and the Word was with God and the Word was God

. And it was that Word that became my Word and my God and it all came together when I started reading his Word that I saw the importance of words and the power of the word to be able to speak the word and motivate with the word and elevate with the word consecrate, dedicate, even create with the word - but I found that I could also exacerbate with the word, and I could also annihilate with the word, and desecrate with the word and even emasculate with the word,

That I had to begin to use words very carefully for I found that there's life in the word

But this knowledge only made my love grow deeper, for how can one word become so many words, like a noun word, a verb word, then an exclamatory word or a commanding word, like Alpha and Omega, Beginning and End, the First and the Last, my All in All- yeah,

Oh how I love the Word- (Pause)

...Tell me have you ever lain in bed at night and the Word would just come and caress your mind and that with every nuance, and every insight and every phrase, and turn of a phrase, where only a certain word would do, uhmmm yeah – that's how it is for me – how sometimes in that very special part of night, when only a few souls are lingering about, just before the day breaks, that a word would just ease into that semiconscious state of mind and it would take root, then take form and then there it would be (pause),

A title for my next play, a new book to be written, and new poem to be spoken,

Oh yeah – I can love his word forever,

Then I am finally able to drift back off, saturated, totally consumed, wallowing in this awesome word.

And later, just a little while later, when I wake up, I lean over the side of the bed, still groggy, remembering, totally spent from the word. So I ask you – got a light?

HIDING IN PLAIN SIGHT
By Elouise D. Woodward

Today is the day I stand in my pain; the feeling of sadness has taken over my domain.

Life in the shadows of others were my comfort zone,
My lack of self-worth consumed me as I stood all alone.
Confession never spoken is bad for the soul; it's traumatizing to know that you had so much of my control. I'm tired of hiding so I must come out for all to see,

I finally found me, I look normal, sound normal, do you agree?
After all the emotional rollercoaster rides you made me believe,
you tried to destroy me in a way you never achieved. Isolation was created to be easily influenced by you; history always repeats itself in how you pursue.

Why did you feel the need to choose me for your pleasure; you
were married to my mom that should have been your treasure.
I held malice in my heart for her lack of knowledge; my trust in God is who I give all the homage. If you can see me now, I am who I want to be;

strong, resilient, independent, caring, and I can finally be free.

All those nights of terror you put upon me; my mind body and soul you couldn't take from thee. You made me hate who I was and drag me around just like a dog on a leash, you wanted to destroy everything associated with me, including my peace.

I yow to remove all the hate I felt inside for a very

long time; what you did to me all those years were overlooked as a crime.

So today I look up and thank God for not leaving me; He said I cast out all those bad memories of trauma, pain, isolation - all cast into the sea!

So, if you ever wonder why I'm still alive, God has kept me through all the chaos and said, "You will Survive." The strength God has given me is what I've been yearning for many years; thank you Lord for not putting too much on me, allowing me to cry good tears.

I'm so much better now than I was locked up in my mind; life has given me a new perspective on what I needed to find. When you look at me you don't see all my lashes and scares; karma is always present when you think secrets will be kept locked up in jars.

You suffered and died a horrible death. I pray you asked God for forgiveness before he had taken your last breath. I need to forgive you so I can move on with my life; I know now that God gave me the strength to finally lay down my fight.

WE WOMEN FAMILY
By Chatone Morrison

A Poet
A Giver
A Gypsy
A Healer
A Beauty
A Tower
And Strength

We sit together. We, Women. We, Family. We, Strangers.
Bruised, red apple hearts
Arranged in crystal bowls
So pretty
You cut away the
Soft brown spot and eat
The sweet white meat.

We sit together. We, Women. We, Strangers.
Shelter our wounds
From inadvertent hurt
Behind the camera
The children
The silence
The indifference
The violence
The poetry and
The grief

We sit together. We, Family of Strangers. We, Women.
Reddened
The embarrassment

The shame
The anger
The insanity
The fear and
The disgrace.

We, Women. We, Family.
Turning our faces away
Instead of staring each other down like
Startled deer leaping over the median
Into high beams and
Evening traffic.

How do we end this Great Seclusion?

Trembling, we must admit to wanting more
And tasting the edge of joy at the sides of our mouths like
A swelling and receding wave at the shore.

Love Is The Only Conclusion.

We sit together. We, Women. We Strangers.
Cast our masks
To the table's center
Raise our eyes to see each other
Raise our glasses
Full of story
Rip off years of apprehension
Together, sip.

We, Women. We, lovers.
Embrace our arms and legs around each other

Kiss each other's tears
Absorb the trepidation
Holding us behind black ropes and chains
400 years
Never calling us by our names.

We come together. We, Family.
Hours fall like steep rain
Disappearing into clouds
And back again
Into the precious cycle of
Wanting. Needing. Sharing. Loving.

Some of us are bruised.
Thrown in corners without our skin.
Private memories alone too much to see.
But, Together
Walls down and finally free
We create a special love
We are Women.
We are Family.
A Poet
A Giver
A Gypsy
A Healer
A Beauty
A Tower
And Strength

September 10, 1999/
· Revised April 1, 2022

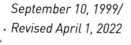

Short Stories

WHAT IS LOVE?
by Annie Veyakhone

My twenty-something year old self would have said that love is giving your all to another person. Being so embodied by this other being and getting caught up in your emotions is what love means. To live, to breathe, to fall helpless in love is the true meaning of love.

But is it?

Eight years ago, I thought I fell head over heels in love with a man who turned out to save my life and I am forever grateful for him for changing my mind and really helping me find the love I have for myself. I invite you to come with me as we reminisce on this heartbreak.

It was the end of September, and the autumn crisp air was starting to get chilly as the sun was setting. I was walking to my then boyfriend's condo and feelings of anxiety and nervousness fell over me as different scenarios went through my head. We had taken a break six months prior, but we wanted to work on our relationship. He had been distant over the phone, but we needed to talk. He opened the door, gave a one arm hug like I was another bro, and we sat down on the couch in front of his tv like we had millions of times before; and while this was familiar, it felt completely different. He didn't leave room for small talk, he told me he didn't see a future for us; that he felt like he was pretending when he was with me, and that sometimes he just didn't want to be around me.

I didn't hear those words. I heard it, but I thought knew that I could change his mind if I just tried a little harder to convince him that he did want to be with me; he just didn't know it yet. I felt beaten when he firmly said no. I was even more devastated after suggesting that we remain friends when he again said that he didn't think it would be a good idea, since he didn't think I could handle it.

That's when I knew it was over and I knew that there was no way in this lifetime that I could change his mind.

A flood of thoughts and emotions ran across my mind and body. What could I have done that was so horrible that he couldn't even stand the sight of me anymore? How could I have missed the warning signs during the last three months that we were together? If he wasn't happy, why didn't he just say so? Why couldn't he just love me like I loved him? Or so I thought it was love.

There were countless questions that just would not stop.

I finally realized he'd been telling me all along that he didn't want to be with me. His actions spoke loud and clear, but I was so involved in trying to change the situation that I didn't see the reality. And that reality was: He just did not want to be with me. Unfortunately, this wasn't the first relationship that I allowed myself to get lost in. So how in the world did this happen to me? Again?

The idea of being in love happened. That's what.
   I wanted that romance, that fairytale. I wanted to finally know

what it was like to be in real grown-up love, and not kiddie, high-school love. I wanted all of that.

I was so tired of always being the bridesmaid and never the bride. I was starting to feel like maybe it just wasn't in the cards for me. And that scared me.

When I finally woke up from this, I started to ask myself, "Who the hell are you, and why did you allow yourself to go through that?" I used to think I was this strong, independent woman who knew exactly what she wanted in life and wouldn't tolerate any BS from anyone.

I was always so proud to list all hundred qualities that my future husband would have, and I told everyone that I was never, ever going to settle. I was all talk but never walked the walk.

After much soul searching, I finally had the courage to put my foot down and say enough is enough. That was when the real challenge began.

Who am I again? I don't even know anymore...
I had to find a quiet spot and re-evaluate me.
I figured out that I'm one person with friends and family, but the complete opposite when I'm in a relationship. I try a lot harder to please; I'm less outspoken, less confident, and less of myself. I was scared to let the real me out in fear that maybe they wouldn't like me.

I was too scared to say no to something that I knew I was against.

I felt like I had to create this façade of someone that was fun, loving, and patient, and what I thought was "perfect" in someone else's eyes. Not saying that I'm not fun or loving or patient; I just tried too hard to be seen that way.

My mistake was not being true to myself—not standing up for myself, not keeping true to my morals, and not loving myself enough to just say no when I wanted to.

I've discovered that I am not flawless and that it's okay to not be perfect. But most importantly, I've learned that it's okay to love yourself first, and if you must lower your standards to get the love that you think you want from someone else, then it's not worth it.

These challenges haven't been easy, but it challenged me to recognize my worth.

And to me, love means to find your happiness, find your passion, and find what resonates the most with you. The meaning of love starts with yourself.

TRANSCENDENCE
By Valerie L. McDowell

That first time I ventured into that West African dance class, I felt at home. My heartbeat instantly connected to the djembe as I moved my body unencumbered, freeing myself, lost in the cadence of the drums.

My former stringent training in pointed toes and elongated limbs, effortlessly fell away into undulating hips and flexed stomps into the tarnished, wood floor.

The cares of the day, all the reports still needing to be done, the responsibilities to and for others, vanquished as I was transported to a destination where only I and the Source of all creativity reigned. The God of the Universe was summoning me in the drums. And in that call and response of the Master Drummer, I was finally at peace and one with my Creator.

The tempo of my heart was now racing with the drummers skillful thundering on the taut skin of the ancient gourd. I closed my eyes as I got low, lazily moving, escaping the frantic pace of my daily life, into the cleansing flow and reverberating movements, like the waves of the ocean cascading against the shore. Easy. Back and forth. Such perfect choreography. No missteps. Just delicate strides as I allowed myself to be gracefully guided into synchronicity with my partner. His arm extended, stretched towards me, pulling me so close; then suddenly propelling me to that place beyond reason and logic where ideas flow freely and time no longer exists. It is all light and joy and peace.

Abundance is all around me.
I came that you might have life.
A more abundant life.
Take my yoke upon you.
Learn of me. My yoke is easy.
My burden is light.
Illumination. Revelation.
Oneness. Harmony.
O, to dance with my Creator.
Divine!

LOVE IS A WARM FEELING INSIDE
by Valrie Yee Logan

All the grades were assembled in a cozy area. Brainstorming, I asked, what is love?

Expecting to hear brilliant minds express themselves, I waited to see many, excited hands, familiar hands, waving like flags, to be called on to give a response?

There was silence. I knew they heard the question. So, I waited, but not for long.

Someone was eager to share and responded. I couldn't see a face. Swiftly, my eyes walked towards the direction, and I listened intently. I realized that the voice was coming from where the kindergarten students stood. So, I listened carefully then I heard a brave, gentle, voice shout, "LOVE IS A WARM FEELING INSIDE!"

Wow! Applause echoed in the air. That was lovely, brilliant! It blew my mind. A definition of love so simply expressed and could be understood by all. This is "truth" expressed by a 5-year-old boy! I was impressed. How did a "babe" know that what he has been feeling is love? Was he hugged, kissed, and told; I LOVE YOU? Did he know he was loved? Did he experience pleasure and comfort from these feelings? I had no doubt, love is a universal feeling. That boy knew what love is - he knew how it feels to be hugged and cuddled, in the arms of those he loved and those who loved him, and that was often, followed with the words I LOVE YOU. He is a genius!

50

This warm feeling is first felt in the family. It is felt by the rich, the poor, and by lovers - whether one day old or ninety-years old. The blind have no eyes yet feel loved, by kind words and deeds. Love can be seen in the eyes. Love can be heard in kind and pleasant voices. It is expressed in heartfelt songs and breath-taking music. It can be tasted in a well-prepared, delicious dish. It can be experienced in a sweet, rejuvenating bath and a special and refreshing drink. Love is felt when kissed, when holding hands, and when getting that needed massage, from caring hands. Yes, Cheryl's love is one she gives, serving others genuinely and thoroughly – completely and freely from the heart which is truly understood by appreciative hearts - rare in the world at large. Valrie listens with her heart and offers help, empowering others to shine. Oh! Maria's hugs - she holds you and everyone so tight, embracing you close to her endearing heart.

Not to mention "that feeling" one gets from the smell of a rose, exotic fragrances, and the aroma of a loved one's perfume. How can we forget a mother's natural scent? Our mothers' arms have been our beds, and there we were all fed; mother's breast was the best.

What about the feeling one's gets holding a baby and looking at its clean, soft skin and fresh, breathtaking smell? Oh, such awe, experiencing God's love from an answered prayer. Also, astonishing moments seeing God's guidance, help, protection, and concluding that this is NO COINCIDENCE. We must, it's vital, love ourselves but not to be self-centered. We should love others – even our enemies. Love strangers too; however, exercise wisdom. Never withhold love from our children. Neither should our love, for our elderly parents, ever grow cold.

Was that a difficult task students, to define that wonderful, well-known feeling – Love? Imagine God's creation, a field of beautiful lilies, or a variety of fruits from which to choose and enjoy. The sun and the rain are vital for life. Also, our bodies are wonderfully made. Jehovah God gave us a wonderful gift - LIFE. He gave us the BIBLE, a source of wisdom, and a lamp for our feet. He gave his only son to die for us, opening the way for "real life"- The hope of living in paradise, a hope that burns brightly in obedient hearts. God's love is "warm" - it's active.

SO, LOVE IS ACTION, DOING; IT IS A VERB, which creates feelings. So, love listens and tries to understand a person's pain, and help. Love empowers others. Love will be there through thick and thin. That is love.

A MEETING IN THE MALL WITH MY FAVORITE MUFFIN
By Linda Jones-Vickers

It was a Thursday morning in March of 1994. My BFF Teresina called and wanted me to pick her up so we could go to the gourmet shop in The Coral Square Mall. We were going to My Favorite Muffin where they made the best homemade muffins ever, especially the cheese muffin. That first bite - So Delicious! It felt like you were falling in love. While we frequently visited this shop, I didn't really feel like going that morning, I had PMS and was feeling crappy. You see I was recently divorced and feeling down and a little sour about life and love. I just wanted to be alone with my thoughts and process my feelings and where I was going in my life. But because she had tried all week to get me out of the house, I decided to take her up on this offer. Yet for some reason I couldn't get myself together and get out of the house. Before I knew it, almost three hours had elapsed since her call. Finally I was into my car zooming down University Drive with my radio blasting music from one of my favorite CD, when this soulful song came on called SEND ME A LOVER. It just touched my heart. The words were so what I was feeling at this time. The specific verses said ... "Send me a lover, someone to believe in, please send me someone that I can hold, send me a lover, a new beginning someone to take away the cold and give me back what I been missing .All the love that lies and waits inside your heart..."

As I sped down the street singing along with the artist, with this beautiful song resonating in my soul, it stirred such deep emotions that by the time I reached my BFF's house I felt better. So when I arrived and because so much time had elapsed, I asked her if she still wanted to go to the mall because it was nearing the noon hour and we had to be at work by 3:00. Nevertheless she was still game, so off we went.

When we got to the mall, instead of going to get our muffins, Teresina suggested that we go window shopping. So as we strolled along viewing the merchandise in theshop windows, this guy walked by and smile and said, Hello. My BFF being who she is, sassy and outspoken, stated look at you not in the mall five minutes and you have men smiling and speaking to you already. I said SO? Let's go get our muffins and coffee so we can eat them and go home; remember we are working this evening.

As we turned around to go back to the gourmet shop, the guy who spoke to us as he passed by also turned around and was walking back toward us with this sexy smile and really cute face. As he approached us, he said Hello again, where are you ladies off to? And My BFF being who she is just started batting her eyes, flirting and telling him about the shop My Favorite Muffin. He asked, mind if I join you? My name is Toby. Teresina stated, yes please join us. Me normally the cool, calm and collect one was tongue-tied and nervous. He maneuvered and got in the middle and walked between us. My heart was pounding and me who never perspires, had a meltdown. Once we arrived at the shop, we made our orders. He offered to pay, but because we didn't know him, we declined. As Toby sat at the table across from Teresina and I talking, he kept making eye contact with me, which made me bashful. Again, me, who was always bold, always in control. He started sharing a little about his life. How he was a private investigator, recently divorced, recovering from a recent injury so he was under doctors care and not working in his field at this time, And of course, my BFF being who she is, had to tell him I was a nurse, where we worked, and that I too was recently divorced. Imagine this, me trying to appear cool and sophisticated, while my heart was pounding, my hands were shaking, and I was perspiring profusely. Every time I looked into his golden-brown eyes, I felt like I was eating My Favorite Muffin. Then it happened. I was so nervous I spilled my coffee. Thank goodness it was just a small one. But I was so mortified. But Toby wasn't fazed at all, he asked for my telephone number and I shared it with him. Of course my BFF, being who she is, told him we had to work the 3-11 shift and I would be finished with my med pass at 9:00 pm. That afternoon when I got to work, everyone on my unit knew I had met this cute guy named Toby, and how he had beautiful golden-brown eyes and pretty hands because not only was he a P.I. but he was a part-time musician who played the guitar. When he was in the military he had did a couple of overseas tours with the band Contrast and even recorded an album which can still be found on YouTube today. Well that night at exactly 9pm, Toby called me, and the rest is history.

From that day to this, we will have been together 29 years as of March 10th. That meeting in the mall led me to My Husband, the love of my life. My Soulmate. But most of all My Favorite Muffin, the kind that makes you feel like you are falling in love. That song SEND ME A LOVER delivered me a lifetime lover, so ladies and gents check it out on YouTube and listen to the words. They are still so beautiful. Even a few other artists have recorded it, but the rendition I love is by Taylor Dayne.

My message to you is, Don't ever give up on love or life. Had I not gone to the mall that day at that specific time, our paths would not have crossed. And I would not have had this beautiful life experience. Toby shared with me that after he spoke and passed by us, something told him to turn around and go back. At the same time, something told me to turn around and go back too. So we both listened and turned back. We met each other in the middle. He said I was just the kind of woman he had prayed for, and I got my prayers answered too. I got My Favorite Muffin, Toby!

OUR AUTHORS

Gerri Aldridge is an author, motivational speaker, mentor, retired special education teacher, a 23-year breast cancer survivor, and loving wife to Michael Aldridge and mother to Karma S. Chacon. She is a co-author in "His Grace is Sufficient" where she passionately gives great advice on how to triumph after tragedy! Gerri is currently working on several collaborations with well-known authors, and other survivors! She holds a M.Ed. from Temple University and the University of West Georgia. You can reach Gerri on fb: Gerri Savage-Aldridge, I.G. therealgerri, twitter sistagerri, email: gerri7328@comcast.net

Betty Badgett, Mother of two adult children, a retired Registered Nurse, and a volunteer at an adult senior day. I have always had a passion for writing and reading. I have had a few short stories published in two journals while living in Upstate New York. Now that I am retired, I look forward to having more time to pursue my dream of writing and someday publishing.

Rocio L. Baker is an educator, author, educational trainer, and ESL consultant. Her years of experience in K-12 classrooms, reading and writing for all grade levels, unveiled her desire to write. An interest that led her to write her first bilingual English/Spanish children's story: Where Is My Rainbow? Dónde está mi arco iris? At present, she is writing a memoir with close guidance from her Book Writing Coach, Valerie McDowell.

Jermain Barnes is a father of two lovely daughters and a son of a God-fearing woman. My mother is the one who believed in me, when I did not believe in myself.

Lynn Brown is a creator, content strategist and lover of the arts. Writing is her first love.

Cheryl Crockett, author, actor, free spirit, poet - sometimes poignant, occasionally militant, frequently wistful, usually humorous, diversely creative... Christian.

Cari Davis is originally from Detroit, Michigan and has been writing poetry since high school. The first person who inspired me to write poetry, besides my mother, was Susan L. Taylor. She was the editor of "Essence" magazine. In each issue she had a column entitled "In the Spirit". I absolutely loved it. It was emotionally driven. My poetry is emotionally driven as well. I write all in my feelings! Good, bad, happy or sad! Authentically me!"

Darlene Gibson is a warm, caring, and loving Christ-centered woman. She is passionate about family, community, and ministry. Darlene is also learning to listen more than she speaks. She is a family advocate, youth mentor, and inspirational encourager to her family, friends, and community. She can be outspoken and anxious at times, but is kind, and strives to be patient with others and herself.

Debrina Hall James is retired from North Carolina State Government. She worked in the mental health field providing community support services to adults and children, assisting them in developing critical living and coping skills as well as achieving and maintaining rehabilitative goals. She holds a B.A. in Business Administration and a M.S. in Human Services/Counseling Studies. She is currently working on her lifelong dream of becoming a published author.

Valrie Yee Logan is originally from Jamaica but has made New York her home. An educator of the highest degree, Ms. Logan has been writing for most of her life.

Valerie L. McDowell is a writer, editor, author, book coach, publisher, and consultant. Her passion is helping first time authors get their stories told and their books published. To find out more, visit her @ www.bookcoachexcel-erator.com

Chatone Morrison, known as The Princess of Positivity® is a lifelong lover of words and poet. She is a confidence coach, a skincare business owner, and author of the book, F.A.T.T. & Happy. She resides in Maryland with her husband Mark and their two children.

Linda Peterson has written everything from short humor to feature articles from poetry to her present work on memoir.

Ozetta V. Posey is a highly-decorated and awarded retired law enforcement professional who loves good conversation and traveling.

Marsha Reeves Jews is a mother, grandmother, and entrepreneur. Her passion and mission are to provide excellence in her small business – Marsha Jews & Company, a company focused on marketing, communications, producing large trade shows, exhibitions, conferences, and jazz festivals. Marsha's passion is her weekly newsletter and live streaming show - WKIM/We Keep It Moving w/Marsha Jews.

Martita Robbins is a happily married entrepreneur and educator. Her purpose in life is to use her talents, passions, and goals to create a harmonious life.

Octavia Smith is a PCA/UA/PSA and Christian who loves to encourage and inspire people by spreading the word of God through ministry. She is the mother of one daughter and loves to cook different types of food, travel and take care of her family. Her most important role is as servant to the Most High God.

Arnita Sydnor is a CNA nurse and Christian who loves to encourage and inspire people. In her spare time she enjoys writing. She is a mother of three and has seven grandchildren.

Sandra Thomas is a native of Panama, Central America. She obtained her formal education in New York and began her nursing career in Brooklyn, NY, first as an operating room nurse, then civilian-military nurse, hospice nurse, and currently as a retired school nurse. As a hospice nurse, Sandra sat at the bedside of her patients and watched them take their last breath while comforting the families. Sandra is currently preparing to become board certified as a Nurse Health Coach. You can reach her at grevealed2U@yahoo.com or visit her website: www.grace-revealed.com

Annie Veyakhone is a native Virginian who is a mom by day, a writer and holistic life coach by night. When she is not prepping meals or playing referee to 3 toddlers, she helps people identify their true passion in life and loses herself in a dystopian society which is the premise of her new upcoming book.

Linda Jones Vickers is a wife, mother, grandmother, and a retired nurse with over 30 years of healthcare experience. A mentor for women and a prayer warrior, she is inspired to make a difference wherever she goes. The ever Optimist, Linda has been an avid reader since childhood, writing poetry and short stories throughout her life. She believes a book is a powerful tool that empowers you with knowledge, skills, inspiration and so much more. Linda also hosts a biweekly telephone prayer-line.

Elouise D. Woodard is an African American poet from Newark, New Jersey. She grew up destitute but maintained a love of poetry, having hid herself from the world because she thought she wasn't good enough. Elouise stuttered as a child and had low self-esteem but concluded that hiding was an excuse for failure; so she straightened her back, and embraced her gift, realizing who she is and what she wants, elevating to the highest level my God will allow.

Made in the USA
Middletown, DE
10 October 2022